WINTER WEAVING
and
Other Poems

WINTER WEAVING

and
Other Poems

LILLIA M. OLCOTT

VANTAGE PRESS
NEW YORK   WASHINGTON   HOLLYWOOD

FIRST EDITION

Published by Vantage Press, Inc.
120 West 31st Street, New York, N. Y. 10001

Manufactured in the United States of America

CONTENTS

Page

Navajo Land   11
Desert Road   11
The Desert   11
South West   12
Weather Wise   12
Desert Jests   13
At Home in May   13
Winter Weaving   14
Green Things Growing   14
Spring Incense   15
Vibrations   15
Lines of Life   16
The Woodland Wakes   16
Only Tomorrow   17
Autumn Evening   17
Beauty of a Northern Spring   17
Country Calling   18
Neighbor Mrs. Wren   19
Dinner Time   19
Bird Neighbors   20
Listen   20
Night   21
God's Hands   21
Secret Melodies   22
Love Ties   22
Sharing   22
Merciful Afflictions   23
Where?   23
The Flower Vendor   24
Goldfinch   24
Rain in the Park   24

Neighbors 25
First Growth 25
Country Twilight 25
Last Dance of the Season 26
Weeds 26
The Builder 27
Song in the Rain 27
Thankfulness 27
Clouds 28
Weft Threads 28
Heirs by Evolution 29
City Fog and Rain 29
Blessing 29
Things to See 30
Dreams Change 30
Love of God 31
Pause Awhile 31
Lullaby 31
Valentine for Mother 32
Impartial 32
Lace 32
Prayer 33
Spinster 33
To Be Fey 33
Because I Love You, Dear 34
Letters 34
The Question Answered 34
Responsibility 35
Spring Cleaning 35
Pictographs 36
Time, the Painter 36
Faith 36
Quilts and Gardens 37
Winter Night 37
Clouds and Hills 38

	Page
The Getting Up of Day	38
Patchwork	39
Revelation	39
A Hollow Reed	39
Indian Petroclyths	40
Western Desert	41
Interference	42
Friend Jim	43
Briars for Kate	45
Changed	48
Time Ticket	48

WINTER WEAVING
and
Other Poems

NAVAJO LAND

Here poetry is woven, lived not read,
The drifting clouds
Draw patterns through the web
Of rocks and sands,
As colors shift and change
By Indian hands.

DESERT ROAD

The tumble weed is rolling across the road today,
The fence wires are matted with brittle weeds turned gray,
The mesquite and the chaparral show not a sign of spring,
Wind whistles over empty space to make the wires sing.
Only ashes of the colors from summer's heat remain;
Yucca spikes and greasewood alone strong hues retain.

THE DESERT

Long stretch of sand that rises mile on distant mile
To mountain buttes of violet and blue;
Torn jagged points of ocher and dark rose
Rise from the nearer space while new
Bright yellow poppies bloom among gray sage,
Uniting hoary past and brilliant present in one view.

SOUTH WEST

Volcanic ash, from fires dead forgotten years
Still blow across this wide spread land
To tinge with silver or with leaden gray
Each hue of living plant; covering rock with sand.

Only the tall yucca racks its piercing blades
And greasewood holds its dark green hue.
The very buttressed towering rocks seem old
Strongholds against the transient and the new.

Then with the silver touch of gusty rain,
All in a day the myriad flowers fling
Ponchos of flaming hues across wide space.
Too brief a time this magic desert spring.

WEATHER WISE

The seamen and the farmers
And those who ride the ranges
Are the ones to whom it matters
How the weather changes,
And therefore scan the sky.
But alert and ever watchful
Are all of those who fly.
It takes a thoughtful man to read
That alphabet on high;
Those constant changing clouds
That form a language of the sky.

DESERT JESTS

At times the desert gaily smiles,
When after rains in early spring
Flowers burst from the sands and fling
Brilliant serapes reaching miles.

Later the desert has an old grim jest
To play on those who venture on her way.
The quivering hot air beckons man away
From the blown track he knows is best.

Strange trees and shade by pools of blue
Seem as familiars to his sun scorched sight:
The saguaro points the way toward left or right
And ocotillo sways as reeds were wont to do.

AT HOME IN MAY

Oh to be at home in May
When the fruit trees bloom,
Snowy plums, rosy peaches,
Pears and apples all atune
With lilting bird notes
And the happy hum of bees.
There, garden spilling over,
Daffodils run through clover
Flaunting their yellow frills
Underneath the fragrant trees.
I am longing for those hills
At home in May, sweet with these.

WINTER WEAVING

The curtains of the air hang thick with frost.
Above the earth a rug is spread of silver, cream and blue
Patterned with arabesque of shade
From trees that lace cold lattices against the sun.
The needle ice hangs motionless, without a stir
Of gleaming thread from a relenting warmth.
Across the sky thin filaments of cloud are spun
For Winter's weaving into gauze to drape
Each weed and bush of quiet fields that rest.
The spinners of the cold are never done,
They always try new patterns on their web,
Designs brocaded with such skill that one
Must breathless marvel at the frosty grace
That wraps the world awhile, then vanishes
To leave a memory of beauty in its place.

GREEN THINGS GROWING

I need to have some green things growing where I am.
I can endure the tread of time's feet better when I know
That I am set upon the way of living things.
Buds of fresh fancies which in time may blow
To tinted blossoms of my working days,
May ripen into fruitful thought and so
Wherever I may be, plant things to grow.
Slight things spring up appearing in a night
But solid growth takes time, seems slow.

SPRING INCENSE

Spring is on the way I see
A purple haze spread on the hills
Where sycamore and hickory
Awaken as the fresh sap fills
Their smallest twigs on high.

Down on the softened drifts of snow
The farm boy drives the laden sled
To where the sap fires flame or glow
And syrup boils in the low shed,
Lifting its incense to the sky.

VIBRATIONS

At times I know we heedless mortals are
Keyed to high notes that seem to come
From some far distant space.
My heart's low beat has caught
The rhythm of an unheard drum;
Then all is well, gladly I take the pace
Of myriad forms of life; a unit in the sum.
That others answer to another note I know:
Full symphony cannot be played alone by drum.
The moon note calls the seas in changing tide
And fish and flesh unwittingly respond
To the same potent spell. What forces may abide
In distant suns we do not know as yet:
Profound the mystery in vibrant spaces wide.

LINES OF LIFE

The rhythm found in shifting dunes are one
With that of wave, or clouds across the sun.
The swirling eddies where swift waters flow
Mark lines the same as knotty pine trees grow.
This curving beauty testifies all life
Is richer when it meets and wins through strife.

THE WOODLAND WAKES

Hepatica is dressed for spring
In silken petals that close fold
Inside a gray soft furry coat
To keep her warm from sudden cold.
The fiddle heads, still tightly curled
Are pushing up from the dark mould.

The alders and the willows wave
With catkins ripe from a warm breeze.
On every bright and sunny day
The sap runs up the maple trees;
But when the frost of night has come
Quick down it slips, lest it should freeze.

The little brooks are free from ice,
Now all the woodland wakes from sleep,
Her winter wraps she puts aside
Remembering a tryst to keep
With spring, who cannot tarry long,
For summer comes on racing feet.

ONLY TOMORROW

Why be afraid to die
So like a child who cries
"I want a light to see to go to sleep."
Then by and by
The tired eyelids droop
And weariness slips off. Why weep
When fresh adventure
Waits the coming day,
Where we may greet
Our dearly loved and make new friends
Along the way?

AUTUMN EVENING

The silver brush of rain brings out color hidden in the
    bark of trees.
There show warm orange browns with black and green
Where all before had seemed but neutral gray.
A rhythmic pattern forms on larger boughs. With silent ease
The ripened leaves drift down till there is seen
Only the branches and a yellow leaf against
The fading turquoise of the ending day.

BEAUTY OF A NORTHERN SPRING

Beauty of a northern spring
Is a fragile tender thing,
Gives promises but will not stay;
Changing like a drift of spray;
Goes dancing off, tiptoes near,
With flash of smile, glint of tear.
Beauty of a northern spring
Is a shy elusive thing.

17

COUNTRY CALLING

I have missed Spring at home this year
The sudden whims of sun and showers
When tiptoe peeping buds appear
To suddenly prank out as flowers.

There when through lingering melting snow
We look we are surprised to see
The flowering snowdrops, row on row
Shake silver bells for the first bee.

And there the crocus suddenly
Blows purple trumpets to proclaim
That it is safe for bloom to be
For surely spring has come again.

The wonder of the waking years
When in the fields, along the brook
From dead brown leaves, the tight green spears
Unfurl to blueflags while we look.

How suddenly we find them there
The flowers that come overnight
And cowslips gleam where all was bare
Like floods of sunshine, pools of light.

NEIGHBOR MRS. WREN

Two inches of rage plus a small perky tail
Machine gun annoyance at me;
Swift darts to the post top, then back to the rail
Fearful her fledglings I'll see.

Fiercely she wonders why I am so rude
Spreading blankets and pillows to air;
Such actions will doubtless disturb her young brood
For Jennie is sure I won't care.

Such swift darting forays for bugs on a vine,
Such chattering scolding at me;
She stutters with rage, there hardly is time
To stuff quiet the mouths of her three.

DINNER TIME

I had some neighbor vireos and they
Most evidently had come to stay.
No sooner was the wide porch table spread
Than vireo would cock a smooth dark head
As if to say "I too dine here today."

When odor of the food spread on the breeze,
Summoning the buzzing fly and bees,
Then vireo and several friends would come,
Sweeping above the table each winged crumb.
We dined together, friendly and at ease.

BIRD NEIGHBORS

My neighbors have a Summer home,
And one for Winter too.
In Summer they lived near my house,
When Fall came off they flew.
Not all the neighbors left here though,
Some stay the whole year through.

Those who stay wear black and white
With various tones of gray,
Far brighter are the hues that clothe
The ones who went away;
The Summer loving songsters
Who like things bright and gay.

All Winter I will feed the birds,
Sparrow and chickadee;
But when there's first hint of Spring
Eager I watch to see
If there's a red vest on the lawn
Or a blue wing in a tree.

LISTEN

Be still my feet that I may catch
The tune the wind is bringing,
Be quiet breath that I may match
The words that tune is singing
To birds that on the air today
Their safe way home are winging.

NIGHT

The opalescent moon is caught
In silver filigree of twigs
To hang against dark satin of the sky;
While frosty wisps of cloud that sought
To veil the light, dissolve in mist
As night winds blow them by.

GOD'S HANDS

Last night I saw God's hands.
The calloused palms were hard,
The fingers worn and scarred
From building suns and earth,
Roads and the homes of men.

And then I saw God's hands
Were only small and white;
Weak, but with such a might
As may serve children,
Or hold the hearts of men.

I know now that God's hands
Are those held out to aid;
That comfort those afraid.
These build a better world:
Strong, tender hands.

SECRET MELODIES

Give heed to sounds until the inner ear
May catch the secret melody each hour brings;
The songs of life, of happiness or pain
That pass by all unnoted if you do not hear;
The muted songs that all of nature sings
For you perhaps but once, or may repeat again.

LOVE TIES

Love is like a cobweb
Spun across our years
Catching dust of daily cares
And bedewed with tears.

Those who brush the web away
Cannot restore a line
So add a new tie every day
To strengthen love with time.

SHARING

With singing heart and eyes that see
Beauty about me everywhere,
I only hope that I may be
Able with those I teach to share;
To open windows so that they
May see what loveliness is there;
To guide their eager hands to do
The world's work in a fine, free way,
Watching them grow in breath of view,
Ready to build for a better day.

MERCIFUL AFFLICTIONS

Long years ago, when I was young
And small griefs came to me
Old mammy said, "Just cry awhile
Then bye and bye you'll see
The Lord sends merciful afflictions."

So many things that seemed awry,
That vexed or hindered me
Have shown where secret treasure hid
So it has often come to be
Blessed merciful affliction.

And as the years have passed along
In many ways I've learned
That strength of soul, true sympathy,
By grief alone are earned.
Blessed merciful afflictions.

WHERE?

Where do the shapes of things go?
Etchings of the frost
Petals of the flower,
Fragile beauty lost after a brief hour;
Where do the shapes of things go?

What happens to the sounds
Of singing bird,
The hum of bees,
Fragments only heard
Like a passing breeze?
What happens to the sounds?

THE FLOWER VENDOR

"Flowers, plants, flowers:" the huckster with his raucous voice
Calls out his wares in dirty city street,
Like catbird swinging in a blossomed apple tree
The harsh notes call the eye to meet
The loveliness of petaled harmony.

GOLDFINCH

Above a field of waving grass
A goldfinch dips and swings,
Like vocal sunshine are the notes
Of the lilting song he sings.

RAIN IN THE PARK

Across the park the lights at dark
Quiver like shaken drops of dyes.
The traffic tower spills down a shower
Of ruddy gleams beneath our feet:
And passing cars weave tinseled bars
All through the carpet of the street.
The storied buildings lighted seem
Patterned like fabrics of a dream.
The city moves all dressed with stars.

NEIGHBORS

Friends gather on my porch and we
Together watch the stars come out
And talk of many things to be
Here in the country round about.

We talk of work, we talk of play,
Of friendly things and simple deeds,
Of books, or journeys far away.
Of empires, and garden seeds.

FIRST GROWTH

See how timidly the little leaves
Steal out to sniff the wind to know
How much of thaw they may expect, or snow,
Only the catkins have appeared so bold,
They know no fear of change to cold.

COUNTRY TWILIGHT

The day is fading and the green
Has crept into the evening sky,
A single star is faintly seen.
The long lake stirs as with a sigh.

A coolness comes down from the hill
Where tall trees all day shadows spread
Above the spring where waters spill
Out over ferns and spearmint bed.

The birds have settled for the night
And only a soft note is heard
As though one dreamed of the day's flight
And sleeping called another bird.

LAST DANCE OF THE SEASON

When Autumn comes piping over the hill
You can see how the tall trees thrill,
Putting their work day clothes away,
Changing to others brightly gay,
For the late gypsy dance of the season.
Maples and sumachs go beyond reason.
The shore willows, crinolined in gold,
Flirt with swamp oaks strong and bold
In dark crimson cloaks today.
In yellow lace blond birches sway.
Only the tall somber pines are seen
Conservatively still in green.

WEEDS

Weeds flourish and they never know
They are not wanted where they grow.
When someone gives them watchful care
They may find a treasure there.
Some will yield a gift of sweet;
Others we find good to eat.
Twisted fibers spun out strong
Hold burdens or may clothe a throng.
Root or stem or fruited pod;
Each was placed there gift from God.

THE BUILDER

It is the builder of dreams
Who reaches a star.
More fragile than gossamer
Those first girders are
But they soar to great heights
As they vault across space.
Strength shows in their motion
Like nature's own grace.
A thought that takes substance,
A dream come alive
With man's trained endeavor
Plus courage to strive.

SONG IN THE RAIN

I heard a small bird singing in the rain,
Then lifted up my heart at what I heard,
For though my life seemed overwashed with tears,
And those I love can never come again,
I have found courage from the singing bird.
I still can smile and hear through all the years
That fairy fluting voice, undaunted sing
Through cold and rain, surmounting all its fears.

THANKFULNESS

Let me be like the small bird
That throbs with song
Regardless of the light;
Who never criticizes dawn
Whether gray or bright:
Gives greeting to the day
After the peaceful night.

CLOUDS

Only those who hold communion with the sky
In spaces unencumbered, wide and free
For all the winds of heaven to blow
May know how wonderful the clouds may be.

The stippled pattern of the pale washed sky,
Faded by winter, in a northern spring.
Swift scudding rags of clouds that blow
Across moon framed in iridescent ring.

Spreading scales of warning mackerel sky.
Black night, sharp stabbed by flash of light like doom.
The blue of velvet tropic night and stars
With hint of houri veil across the moon.

The piling thunderheads above the bars
Of jagged mountain rims beyond the plain.
The heavy hanging bags of leaden gray
That sag until they tear to spill the rain.

The startling sunburst at the end of day
With purple streamers from a blazing sea.
The lowery dawn, as though the night would stay.
Men learn how wonderful the clouds may be.

WEFT THREADS

We are the weft threads
Evolving the pattern of our time;
Dull or bright as we live our parts
Of the rhythm in the great design.

HEIRS BY EVOLUTION

Through the long ages past God built our frame
From a small shapeless atom, drifting in a sea.
By countless changes the evolving form
Has reached its present stature. Let there be
The knowledge that all life is one, no change
May quench the spark, His gift throughout eternity.
Heirs not alone of flesh but of the spirit light.
Clearer the soul may shine, clearer the eye shall see.

CITY FOG AND RAIN

Gray drifts of rain across the city pass
Blending to color harmonies like marshland grass
The reeded shafts of stone and brick,
Then as the stormy night shuts off the sky
From far below the lights gleam out and try
To cut with man-made stars, the fog grown thick.

BLESSING

Let me give thanks that it is there,
Plenty and enough to share:
Light, not blinding, but for sight,
Shelter for rest in quiet night,
Water and food to spare;
Warmth of hearth and human heart,
Work in which I take my part,
Life and love, joy and pain,
Lord, I thank You once again.

THINGS TO SEE

Did you ever, on a hot and sultry day, when climbing up a
    thickly wooded hill,
Catch your breath in wonder, as you came upon a clump of
    ivory coral-fungus, statue still?
Did you ever chance to find forget-me-nots growing wild in a
    swale, like pools of blue,
And briary tangled thickets of swamp roses, like prickly pink
    islands breaking through?
Did you ever, in late winter, see thawing frozen apples on a
    bough,
And trimly tailored waxwings uproarious, in a wild, hilarious
    row?
Did you ever of a morning waken early, in your blankets wet
    with dew,
To look right at a rabbit, who was every bit as much astonished
    as were you?
Did you ever see a high and shaley cliff hung with swinging
    silent bells of columbine?
And a little brook that sparkled into space, falling like a
    tasseled necklace of springtime?
With a world so full of lovely things to see I wonder what's
    around the turn of time.

DREAMS CHANGE

It does not seem that I can bear this year
To have late autumn winds blow down the hill,
For like the summer leaves my pulse grows slow;
I almost feel the touch of winter's chill.
The dreams that were so full of life and dear
Are gone and may not come again I know;
Yet when the seasons bring the miracle of snow
There spreads another page on which to write
Life's song in gold and blue against the white.

LOVE OF GOD

If to my heart the love of God has shown
His tenderness and mercy for his own,
Then must I help some other soul afraid
Of that dread dark they cannot see beyond;
That they may trust and undismayed
May live in life, nor feel alone.

PAUSE AWHILE

I know not where nor when and how to go,
But I will close my tired eyes awhile
With faith that You will show my way to me.
Worry and fear are briars on the path and so
I pause until Your guidance sets me free
From hindrance. I will draw nearer Thee.

LULLABY

Safe in the little nest
I've prepared for you
Baby take your rest
When down drops the dew.

Now the birds slumber,
The butterflies sleep
Gulls without number
Are rocking on the deep.

Safe on your mother's arm
Dear baby lie.
Safe from all earthly harm,
Bye baby bye.

VALENTINE FOR MOTHER

They wrote their valentines of yore
To dimples and to youthful grace;
My dear had all of these, but more;
She has a love look in her face.

She has a spirit that shines through
Her eyes, that seem to her so dim;
And willing hands that ever do
Kind deeds, and faith that trusts in Him.

I wish that I might let her know
How much her courage strengthens mine,
But I can only love her, so
I choose her for my valentine.

IMPARTIAL

Sweet briar roses
Opening in the sun
Offer their fragrance
To every one.
Young child or hobo
Matters not to rose.
Offering beauty
Is why it grows.

LACE

The most beautiful lace
Is like dainty ferns
Spread over with cobwebs fine;
No one has excelled the witching grace
But follow on nature's line.

PRAYER

Dear God, I pray that I may be
Of service to some little one,
To help his shining eyes to see
That beauty is a gift from Thee,
A last love touch to work well done.

SPINSTER

She took her heart, so long ago,
And wrapped it up with care,
With silver bars from shoulders wide
And dreams that promised fair.
She folded it in a lacy veil
With plans for a wedding day,
Then on the top shelf of her life
She laid it safe away.
Now young girls tell her of their loves
Sure that she their joy will share
For roses bloomed once in her life
And the fragrance still is there.

TO BE FEY

It is well to be a trifle fey,
If only for the gleam
Of things unknown to other men,
The singing and the dream.
To sense the things that never were,
Or so far have not been.
To look down on a line of years
A cobweb to a star,
To show how things to come
May be fashioned from those that are.

BECAUSE I LOVE YOU, DEAR

Because I love you, dear,
I find I have the faith to wait and pray,
To do the little tasks of every day
All patiently and with good cheer.

Because I love you, dear,
I watch the postman on his rounds each day.
I watch him come; but should he pass, I pray
That God will guard and let you feel Him near.

LETTERS

skirts are short and hats are small
and the sentences, I note,
are not like the ones we wrote
with letters short and tall.
capitals are out of style!
the new letters that we see
have a uniformity:
so I wonder as I smile,
when grandma looks like little sue
do letters feel the same way too?

THE QUESTION ANSWERED

There was a question in my mind.
How did it come to be
That I, who built and own this house,
Find now the house owns me?

Sometimes I have even pondered
The worth of work and strain,
But when I have been long from home
How good home seems again.

RESPONSIBILITY

A part of the great universe you are,
Though less than ripple on time's mighty sea.
Then think, if what you are today was not,
Perhaps the plan for this world could not be.
How other lives touch yours you may not know,
Nor how you sway them towards their destiny.
So walk with strength, but with a humble heart,
With faith as guide on your appointed way:
Apart from all, but with all else a part;
A tool for God to use again today.

SPRING CLEANING

The sky has washed its windows
To let the sun shine through,
Hung fluffy clouds upon the line
To show against the blue.
The wind has brushed old leaves away
In making room for new.

The melting snow has scoured
All wayside ditches clean,
And pebbles in our little brook
Are polished to a sheen.
Robin in his new red vest
Stands awhile to preen.

PICTOGRAPHS

Gently the crystal air sways desert mallow stalk
Against the weathered rock where sunshine warms the stone
Marked centuries ago by Indian hands, long dust.
Green gold of lichens stains the signs, nor mock
With soft erasure, any thought of man's short stay:
But rather say that all things change in time. We must
Perceive the desert sown and harvest grown
Where now the sage brush and the mallows sway.
All things must wax and wane, vanish to come again.
Man's sign upon the rock endures. We know
Peace followed wars, forgotten long ago.

TIME, THE PAINTER

Time weathers wood upon the farm.
Wood bare or painted, either one,
Whether on fence rail or on barn,
Changes by wind and rain and sun.

First bright hues soften, fade, and there
Time works its wizardry on these
Until with brush of rain and air
They blend like bark on living trees.

FAITH

I do not know, nor do I always seek to find
The whys and wherefores of my simple faith,
For deeper than my finite mind
The knowledge of my soul expands in space
To sense God's presence in each ray of light
Attained by any creed or race.
His law for me, to seek him, and be kind.

QUILTS AND GARDENS

Grandmama's quilts and grandmama's garden
Have something in common you know.
Patches of color forming a pattern,
Planned row upon orderly row.

Calico phlox or cloth with sprig printing,
Bright treasure from neighbor or kin,
Each bit recalling some one she knew well.
Fabric or plant, all fitted in.

WINTER NIGHT

The opalescent moon is caught
In silver filigree of twigs
To hang against dark satin of the sky;
While frosty wisps of clouds that sought
To veil the light, dissolve in mist
As night winds blow them by.
A witchery evoked by winter frost
Replaces loveliness of summer lost.

CLOUDS AND HILLS

Why should we fret with our small passing ills?
Lifting our eyes to the high drifting clouds
Changing and passing, see the towering hills,
Shadowed at times, unmoved and strong to stand
Sheltering within their folds this fertile land.

THE GETTING UP OF DAY

I like to bank my pillows high
And watch the ever changing sky,
To see the silver of the lake
Turn opal with the sun awake.
To watch the cloud forms as they pass
Trailing their shadows on the grass,
To see the cobwebs lacy fine
Spread out all bright with dew to shine.

I hear the gossip of the trees
Answered by ripples, as the breeze
Blows softly down the wooden hill
Where the long curving lake lies still.
I hear the cow bells, tinkling clear,
Come from high pastures and draw near.
Oh then I like to lazy stay
And watch the getting up of day.

PATCHWORK

Like old time crazy patchwork
Has modern life become;
Time in little smitches
Held by running stitches;
And some folks call that fun!

REVELATION

I thought all beauty in my garden gone,
With the last blossom dead from winter cold.
Close drawn the curtains to shut out the dark
That so oppressed. Now in the morning I behold
Snow crystal-ferns and flowers bloom.
A living beauty that but changed in hue
From bright warm colors into whites.
Without the seeming death I had not known
That there could be this sign of immortality
In forms that on transparent pane
Bring to me closer still the true reality
Of growing beauty that God's finger writes.

A HOLLOW REED

Unless someone had learned
To play the flute
The hollow reed
Had been forever mute
And thrown away.
That human breath controlled
Brought blessings manifold
And musical today.

INDIAN PETROCLYTHS

Who was the man who carved these signs
On this heavily lichened stone?
What did he mean that seemed so clear,
But to us is all unknown?

What were his goals and what his dream
As he toiled near his camp below?
If we only knew what he really meant
In the days so long ago.

Did his Shaman dream that the Thunder Birds
Would practice learning to fly,
Trailing their shadows over this rock?
Could he faintly imagine why?

He wanted to share what he came to know,
For he sensed he was not alone,
So he carved his signs for others to read
On the long enduring stone.

Out in this land of open space
Somehow it seemed to be
That even then it had come to men,
The need to be strong and free.

WESTERN DESERT

He who wrote of the desert gray and dreary
Must have recalled the drawn out day, when weary
By a long journey under heat of sun,
And plodding toil toward distant goal that won
Such a short gain it well might seem
He struggled forward, thwarted as in dream.

Here on the desert nothing stays the same
Except the verities of life, the frame
On which the Gods have built
Rocks, wood and shifting silt.
Ashes of flaming rock from a far past
Now lightly blow to soften hues too bright to last.

As sunsets blaze in shifting glories to the sight
Beauties unbearable for long: the night
Soon shuts them off to spare the eyes.
Treasures of memory. A fresh surprise
The morning brings, no days alike but all
Offering sunrise for us to recall.

Range beyond bulwarked range may run
The gamut of the living colors from the sun;
Primrose to orange, amethyst to blue,
Rich reds to violet, green, each hue
Holds place but a short time, then changes
As sun moves east to west beyond the ranges.

INTERFERENCE

Hosea was cross, his temper sorely tried
Because the family would interfere
With him and tell him what he ought to do.
He, a grown man and old enough to know
His business better than his children could.
Why all winter he had looked forward to a good lake swim;
And now the water was too cold, they said
The mile across the bay too far for him!
They could not know what a strong man may do.
Here he was, six foot one and built to match
And every year since he had turned eighteen
He swam across and back each summer day.
No tub made you feel clean and fresh with strength
As did the flowing water out of doors.
Young folks now days lacked gumption, they were slack
And put no vim in either work or play.
His Jim would chase a ball across the hills,
And Katie would play bridge all afternoon;
While neither one was much past sixty yet.
It riled him up when they said he was old
And shouldn't overdo himself this year.
Land sakes alive! what was a man to do?
He had been active all his life and now
They seemed to think him old at eighty five
When he was good for ten years more, at least,
And felt as spry as any one around.
Old was he old! he'd show those young ones yet.

FRIEND JIM

We had had Spring for several weeks, warm days
That with strong winds had dried the roads
Enough so that ten days or so before
I had, with chains of course, gone to the lake
To see if things came through the winter well
Or whether there would be much work to do
At mending walls or fixing up the paths:
Whether the mice and squirrels had come in
To start their homemaking, without me there
To warn them out to find another place.
My good old neighbor Jim came up to talk
About the many things that winter brings.
He had been ill, he had a little cough
His sinewed six foot height seemed very thin.
Now with the Spring at hand he would be well
And when the ground was dry enough would plow,
But we could put my posies in he thought:
We planted phlox and pansies, candy tuft,
And planned how all the garden should be made;
The vegetable beyond the flower beds.
Jim said I made him think of early days,
His mother liked such flowers round her yard.
Those peonies by the fence had been hers
And the snowball bush and old spices roses
The fox gloves, larkspur, lemon lilies, all
The old-fashioned flowers that I grew
Reminded him of when he was a lad
Seventy odd years ago come summer.
His brothers didn't care much for flowers,
He like the pretty things, to watch them grow
There in the yard or up along the woods
Where foam flowers and spring beauties were.
We had a good long talk, an afternoon.
Planting or sitting on the steps, he told
About the old farm and the early days

Of Oklahoma, the wild rush to stake
A homestead out, and then of drifting on;
Of mines, and camps and then of home again.
We sometimes had such visits Spring or Fall
Or waiting for the rural mail to come
On rainy days in summer. We were friends.
And so Jim gave me some of the wisdom
Gathered through many years in many lands.
For Jim had seen the world, not always well
But always with a swinging zest in life
That made him wise and skilled in many things.
Some say he is good stock that's run to seed.
That he is a slack farmer—lazy sort
Who'd rather go afishing any day
Than see his crops are in and buildings up.
But Jim, I think, shows wisdom, seventy
Years of work earn anyone loafing time.
He shows the struggle on through briar patches
Unspoken of in his climb up time's hill.
Deep lines are on his face, but his heart is sweet
As a good russet apple in late Fall.

With roads of clay and the long hills to climb
I had to start back early to get through
Before night found me off the main highway.
Jim watched me go. I waved good-bye to him.

Today—last night—and for three days before
The rain has whipped like hail across the panes.
The streams are full and bottoms out of roads.
But just a little while ago there came
A message in a deep voice choked with grief.
Joe said "Jim's gone—He'd like for you to come."
"We bury him on Thursday, up at Scott."

In this cold rain, when Jim loved Summer so!

BRIARS FOR KATE

Kate lived alone; her small unpainted house
Close by the road, as though to watch who passed
And bid them stop to have a friendly word.
Still there was something there that spoke of fear:
The curtains drawn so close against the glass,
The door left just ajar, briar tangled grass,
The barriers through which you felt her peer
Out at the world as though she wished to know
How to be friends, but never found the way.
Kate groped and struggled all her long life through
While her dark eyes showed hurt bewilderment.
The children ran from her and hid themselves,
Or formed in little groups to stand and jeer
And call her Crazy Kate or Kate the Dumb.
They are so heedless cruel when they're young!
The older people too withdrew from her
Because she seemed so strange to them. Her tongue
Had never learned to form words they could know,
Made such harsh sounds: such frenzied breaking through
To human intercourse: for Kate was dumb.

I am so shamed to think that once I flinched
When Kate called to me when I first moved there.
I did not know and the horrific sound
Caught me so unaware I started back,
Then saw her eyes and smiled: Thank God
I had a chance to glimpse her heart through them.
She knew such lovely things. She showed me where
The partridge hid her nest, and when the young
Were startled, where they hid right in plain sight.
She lifted little lambkins up with care,
Such wobbly little fellows could not stand
Unless they leaned against their mother's side.
She was so tender with all helpless things;
But when she visited the country store

She strode along with angry sullen glare
Lest any laugh at her. She hated that.
I think the others hated it as well.
It came, a sudden clutching at the heart,
Then when they laughed the tension somehow broke,
But they were left mute, like herself, with shame.
She looked so strange, with hat no woman should
Ever have worn, it hid her comeliness,
And flapped above her like the wings of bats.
Her clothes were clean but of that sad dark gray
That clouds are when the wind is threatening
The summer hail that beats the young crops low.
Then always she seemed harried, blown about.
Basket on her arm, she would help herself
To what she needed: spread her money out
Upon the counter, grab up her change and go,
With horrid guttural chokings on her way.
Hurting and hurt. They could not understand.
For all her deadened dress Kate loved bright hues
And had an eye to see and find them right.
One day when I was hooking a rag rug,
With all my rolls of cloth which were spread out,
She clapped her hands like any child to see
The bright gay balls roll out along the floor.
She held her breath to watch me pull them through
To make the pattern blossom in the rug.
I never knew when she would next appear.
When painting in the upper pasture lot
I heard a branch snap, she was standing there
Intently watching every stroke I made.
She bent her head, then stretching out her hand
She pointed to a spot of paint and picked
A bit of aster that was growing there
To hold it up and show the needed hue
Where distance blued the hills so far away.
The summer passed, we often met and smiled
With wave of greeting on the road or field.

In winter I was busied in the town
So lost touch with my neighbors in the hills.
Only by chance the doctor thought to say
"Oh by the way, have you heard Kate is dead?"
I could not think at first which Kate he meant.
She seemed strong, and vital as the hills.
I questioned till he told me what he knew.
The boys went rabbit hunting; when they passed
Her little house seemed still and so forlorn.
No smoke curled from the chimney, which was strange
On such a cold day, and the snow about
Her door was white and drifted, not trod down
By any foot in passing in or out.
They rapped and listened, thought they heard a moan
And entered to find Kate there all alone.
The fire was out, but we shall never know
Whether a spark flew out upon her dress
As she sat drowsy in her rocking chair,
A candle fell, or how it came about
But there she lay—not dead—but burned past help.
They did all that they could to ease her pain.
Doctor said he was with her at the end.
She was so restless, rolled her head and tried
With every sound she knew to tell her need.
At last her son came—she was still, so still.
She held his hand and looked and looked again
Her dark eyes tender with her mother love
That kept her quiet. Blessing in her way
The son she would spare any pain she could,
So that she took the queenly part of her,
Her great dark eyes, and let them speak the love
That held her silent till she quiet died.

CHANGED

I looked through my window,
My garden was dead,
When I woke in the morning
I found there instead
Tall ferns and frost flowers
Etched white on the glass
Preserving the forms
Of the blooms that had passed.

TIME TICKET

How little any of us think,
Watching the world as though
We sit to look and blink
At flickers in a movie show.
No holding to constructive thought
To build a firm sure way
From now to then: as though one bought
Rights to throw a mind away.